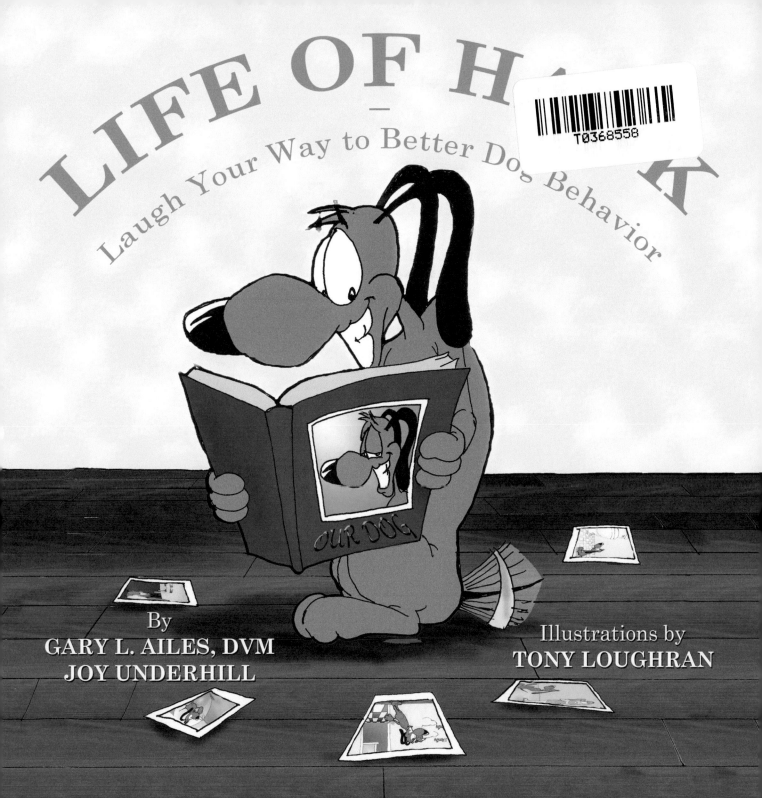

LIFE OF HANK

Laugh Your Way to Better Dog Behavior

OUR DOG

By
GARY L. AILES, DVM
JOY UNDERHILL

Illustrations by
TONY LOUGHRAN

AuthorHouse™
1663 Liberty Drive
Bloomington, IN 47403
www.authorhouse.com
Phone: 833-262-8899

This book is printed on acid-free paper.

ISBN: 978-1-6655-0906-0 (sc)
ISBN: 978-1-6655-0905-3 (e)

Library of Congress Control Number: 2021917398

Print information available on the last page.

Published by AuthorHouse 08/17/2021

authorHOUSE®

Dedicated to Anthony "Tony" Loughran, 48, who passed away suddenly on April 2, 2018 in Kansas City, MO. Tony was born on March 23, 1970 in Charleston, SC to Donald and Lynn Loughran. He was funny, happy, and enjoyed spending time with his family and friends. Tony was an amazing father and husband who was dedicated to his daughter, Gwen, and his wife, Beth. Tony was also a brilliant artist and illustrator. He illustrated two award-winning publications, *Happy Tails* and *You're Having a Wonderful Childhood*.

Tony served bravely in the United States Army and was deployed to Korea. While serving his country, he received the Army Achievement Medal.

AND

Dedicated to all dogs that have given unconditional love and wonderful memories to their human parents.

Contents

Acknowledgements

I t was a pleasure to work with a group of talented, creative and knowledgeable people who became my friends.

Through the miracle of technology, we created this book via email. Dr. Ailes and myself in Nevada, Joy Underhill in New York and Tony Loughran in Florida. The idea to write a book from a dog's perspective with humor was a labor of love.

With Tony's passing, I contacted his wife, Beth and she has helped us with this book to colorize some of Tony's drawings. The original title "Happy Tails – Hilarious Helpful Hints for Dog Owners" was published in 2004.

All parties involved in the revision of the book have given permission to forward all proceeds of the sales to Feeding Pets of the Homeless® of which I am the founder and president.

Thank you for your support,

Genevieve Frederick

FEEDING
PETS®
OF THE HOMELESS
– SINCE 2008 –

Hank's Creators

left – Genevieve Frederick, Tony Loughran, Dr. Gary Ailes and Joy Underhill in New York City for a Ben Franklin Award for "Humorous Book" category.

Genevieve Frederick is the architect of *Happy Tails,* bringing together the writers and the illustrator to create the book and then have it published. The book was awarded an IBPA Benjamin Franklin Winner for Humor in 2005, in New York City. The book has been updated to keep up with medical advances.

After that visit to New York City, the images of homeless individuals, living on the street with their dogs would not leave her mind. She wondered how they found food for their dogs.

At her home in Nevada, Genevieve called food banks that already served the homeless and simply asked them if she could provide donated dog and cat food, would they make it available to their clients. They answered with a resounding, "Yes!" That was the beginning of a long journey to start the nonprofit Feeding Pets of the Homeless® and to watch it grow to become the only national organization of its kind.

In time, emergency veterinary care and wellness clinics were included to provide free vaccinations and basic exams. It also became apparent that homeless shelters needed sleeping crates so the homeless and their pets could have shelter with the added opportunity of working with a social worker to get out of homelessness.

From the onset, the successful coordination, implementation and monitoring of these programs has been due to dedicated staff, volunteers and supporters.

www.petsofthehomeless.org

Creators

 **G**enevieve Frederick is the creator of *Happy Tails*. She had a career in sales and marketing before retiring in 1998. She was the owner of a number of companies. She published two books. She has volunteered her time as a board member of the local hospital foundation to raise funds for a cancer center. She has been a member of Rotary International since 1996 and a past board member on a local level. With her experience, she brings organizational skills, accounting, event management, public relations and publishing expertise.

Since 2006, Genevieve has researched homeless with pets and has spoken to homeless people about their pets. The nonprofit she founded, Feeding Pets of the Homeless®, is the first and one of a few national animal organizations focused completely on feeding and providing emergency veterinary care to pets of the homeless.

Frederick is an authority on the topic of pets and their homeless owners and the human/animal bond. Frederick, representing the nonprofit, has been interviewed on TV, as well as numerous radio shows. She has been interviewed and quoted in a number of books, magazines, blogs, podcasts and other news outlets in the US and abroad.

 **Dr. Gary L. Ailes** is a veterinarian who has worked in the field since graduating in 1972. He is currently the President of the State Board of Veterinary Medical Examiners in the state of Nevada. He is a TPLO Certified Veterinarian, a member of the American Veterinary Medical Association, American Animal Hospital Association, Association of Veterinary Orthopedics for Research and Education, Veterinary Orthopedic Society and the Veterinary Surgical Laser Society. He was featured in the April 1999 issue of *Veterinary Economics*. He has worked consistently to improve himself and is especially skilled in orthopedic surgery. He performs such procedures as Total Hip Replacement, Tibial Plateau Leveling Osteotomy, Triple Pelvic Osteotomy, and other surgical procedures. He has been in partnership with Dr. Woodrow J. (Woody) Allen since 1974 and has built one of the premier practices in northern Nevada.

Outside of veterinary activities, Gary is a past president of the Rotary Club of Carson City. He is an instructor in the Carson City recreational ski program. He coached soccer at the youth and high school level and his core summer team went on to a state championship. He was a member of the Carson City School Board of Trustees for 12 years and president for 3 years. He has been and continues to be involved in numerous other civic activities.

Joy Underhill is an award-winning writer and photographer who lives in upstate NY. Her articles have appeared in numerous publications and she has authored four non-fiction books. She is also owner of a commercial writing firm that specializes in technical content, instructional design, and training videos. Joy enjoys spending time with family, biking, travel, and learning piano in her spare time.

Tony Loughran was a freelance illustrator starting in 1994 until his untimely death in 2018. His main specialty was humorous illustrations and cartoons. Tony illustrated for the Pace University Basketball team, various underground bands, was his Army unit's illustrator where he designed Company mascots, and he had illustrated several children's books.

A Note From Hank

Hank? Hank who?

Hank the dog, that's who.

I know what you're thinking: a dog can't write a book. True enough. I have to admit I didn't bark these words into a tape recorder or click them into a computer using these cute little round paws that I hate to have you touch.

But if you've ever loved a dog, you'll know that we can tell you exactly what we're thinking without uttering a single word. Kind of a cool skill, huh? I mean, we just put a gleam in our eyes, wag our hind ends, jump around and bark, and somehow you humans figure out what we're trying to say. Now if you could just figure out how to communicate that well with your human companions, you just might get somewhere.

Anyway, welcome to my world. You may find it looks just a little like your world, too.

What People and Dogs are Saying About Happy Tails

This book is written by my best friend Hank and a few of his human friends. Hanks was always a real charmer, I recall the time he stole Terri's thong underwear and danced all over the neighborhood with them wrapped around his neck. What a hoot! Or the time he and I found a dead seagull and rolled, and rolled on it until we really smelled good. Hank is pretty lucky to have great humans to care for and love him. Of course, Hank has the "pathetic look" perfected and harly every gets a scolding. Hope you enjoy the book as much as I did." – Tin Cup (The great, great, great, grant grandson of Rin Tin Tin

Dr. Ailes has outdone himself once again. He is so multi-talented and his book is a vivid, humorous, entertaining, tale (or should we say "tail"?). With today's uncertainty of how to properly care for animals, Dr. Gary Ailes, simplifies and enlightens the reader with this very informative, yet light reading book. – Lynda & Kirk Gillaspey, volunteers at the Lake Tahoe Wildlife Care Rehab Center. They are licensed in caring and rehabbing wildlife and are also certified in homeopathic remedies for wildlife.

"A humorous, cartoonish, and informative account of a dog's life from the dog's perspective, including mention of many of the important issues that arise for dogs and their owners. Throughout the book Dr. Gary chips in with helpful and accurate veterinary advice. This is a fun book that adults and children will enjoy as they learn more about how to care for their pup." – Nicholas H. Dodman, Director of the Behavior Clinic, Tufts University School of Veterinary Medicine, and author of *The Dog Who Loved Too Much; Dogs Behaving Badly;* and *If Only They Could Speak.*

 xvii

Hank, Terri, Ron, Munchkin, and Sissy.

Dog, Mother, Father, Baby, and She-Devil Cat-from-Hell.
Notice the structure of this family. Memorize it. Never forget who's the boss and we'll get along just fine.

Ready to learn more?

Hank

Ever since our gifted species crawled near your campfires, we of the canine persuasion have been trying to communicate with

 xviii

you. In my own pack, I'd almost given up hope. It's incredible to think that ye of such impressive cerebral cortex could be so hopelessly ignorant about your most loyal of companions.

I know you love me. Putting fake antlers on my head at Christmas is a sure sign that you think I'm a member of the family, but can you honestly say you understand me? Can you tell by a simple tail wag if my inner pup needs attention or if my bladder is nearing capacity?

If not, keep reading. If so, keep reading anyway. You'll be sure to see yourself—and your pup—on some of these pages.

Terri

The best thing about Terri is that she's easily trained. She's the one to feed me, check the water bowl, take me to the vet, and let me walk her. All I have to do is utter the meekest whimper and she's looking for clues, wondering what I want.

Terri's into home décor—shabby chic with a touch of Feng Shui, to be exact—and her only vice is sneaking a handful of Hershey's Kisses around 4:00 every afternoon. She likes to work out to yoga tapes, which makes for interesting viewing from my perspective.

When Ron's out and the baby's asleep, she's apt to curl up with a book and light a half dozen candles. She calls it "aromatherapy." I call it a good cover for all the lived-in smells I love around here.

Ron

Ron thinks he's king of his castle. Terri and I know otherwise, but why spoil his fantasy? We let him putter around with his big yard machines and he stays happy. Seems like a fair trade for letting us run the show.

In fact, the yard is his main passion, after chicken wings doused in Rigor Mortis hot sauce. Over the years, he's stuffed the garage with two riding mowers, a hedge trimmer, leaf blower, weed whacker, edge trimmer, three rakes, and four thousand trash bags he got on sale. He's also got a good start on his own Ortho chemical factory.

Just one thing, Ron. Dogs and fertilizer don't mix. This should be a no-brainer, but Ron didn't think about how I go barefoot… and then lick my paws… and then pace at the door with a wicked case of the runs.

Please Ron. Turn on the sprinkler and get that fertilizer soaked in well. Save your cream-colored carpet from my onslaught.

Munchkin

I have only one question about undersized humans: Why do you bother having them? Can't you just pick up one partially grown, like you do at the animal shelter? You must have incredible patience or be the world's biggest suckers to raise your litters.

Terri and Ron are just enamored with this little pest. They have at least a dozen pet names for him that will be highly embarrassing if they're still using them when the kid's sixteen. Imagine… the poor boy brings home his first date and they wave goodbye, saying "Don't be home late, Little Poo Poo!"

I guess they have to like him in order to pass along their designer genes, but I can't find much endearing about him. I keep walking up to him with a Frisbee in my jaws, but the kid just drools on the carpet. For right now, he'd rather nibble on my kibble—or my right ear! —when his parents aren't looking.

Sissy

Oh yeah, the cat. I hate cats.

If I threw up hairballs on a regular basis or brought home the liver of some poor chipmunk as a trophy, I'd be evicted in a heartbeat. The only thing she's mastered that I haven't is the ability to make deposits in the loo. I get crazy with envy whenever she scores points with Terri.

I just hate cats.

1

Getting Started

Love at first sight!

Yep, that's Mom in the stirrups there. I'm just a squiggle on the screen—one of eight squiggles, to be exact. Terri posted this shot on the frig until the day they brought me home. She had everyone convinced that they were expecting the munchkin, which wasn't the case yet.

I kid you not—dogs do have ultrasounds—and not just in California. Imagine the thrill of knowing if your home will be filled with four—or fourteen!—puppies. It's a little easier to tell just how blessed you'll be by taking an x-ray at about 42 days, but an ultrasound is fun and it does show if the pups are healthy.

If I may wax nostalgic, these days of uterine bliss must have been the best, even if I can't remember them. Always enough chow.

No drafty nights. No annoying brother tugging at my ear. Not a single potty-training accident!

Dr. Gary Says... Dogs grow up a lot faster than humans. Look at what happens in just 18 months.

At birth to two weeks, I'm just like a human baby: My mom is my biggest influence. I can taste, feel and touch.

At two to four weeks: I'm still most influenced by Mom, but I'm starting to notice my siblings. My eyes open. My hearing and smell develop, and I'm starting to grow teeth. I begin to waddle around, wag my tail, and bark. As soon as I make a mess, mom cleans it up with whatever she has handy (oh yuk... we won't go there!).

At six weeks, I'm just like a human toddler: I can see well. I'm starting to have a social life with other dogs and people. I begin to play and explore my world. My siblings and I are learning what it means to be a dog. I'm getting more coordinated. Weaning begins.

I'm ready to be adopted at six to eight weeks, depending on my genetics. This is the best time to adopt as the pecking order has not developed, yet.

At ten weeks: I can use all of my senses fully. You can begin house-training. I learn what fear is. (Funny how that follows house-training!) I begin to chew as a way of exploring

my surroundings. I'm beginning to adapt to the litter pecking order.

At three to six months, I'm just like a child: I'm most influenced by my siblings and other pets. I'm getting even more curious. I'm beginning to pay more attention to people. I'm teething more and will begin to chew. I'm starting to rank myself with "the pack," including humans, which makes this a great time to start short training sessions. I can move away from Mom, depending on my breed.

At six to eighteen months, I'm your worst nightmare—just like a human teenager: My pack is my biggest influence. I may think that I can challenge humans. I begin to think about sex (unless I'm spayed or neutered).

From Runt to Grunt

Some men have to learn the hard way that having a new puppy is not like having a new baby. For instance, take Ron.

Within a day of my much-awaited birth, Ron invited his poker buddies over for a few rounds of beer. He passed out cigars, lit up, and pulled out a snapshot of me as a newbie.

"Just look at those paws, guys. He's gonna be huge, I tell you. Huge!" Ron's friends just rolled their eyes. I was the puniest runt any of them had laid eyes on. Ron was beaming. "I may even tear out the security system this weekend!"

"Yeah, right Ron," said his best buddy, dealing out a poker hand. "Texas hold'em Cujo, ante up."

The truth was, I was the runt of the bunch. I barely had the strength to push for my place at Mom's 'round-the-clock dairy. But I made up for lost time, and within a couple weeks I looked like a bobble toy with hair. I'd get so milk-drunk that all I could do was let out an involuntary groan after eating. That's how I earned the dreaded nickname "Grunt."

It was Terri's Aunt Ida who saved me from that crippling social disability. "Terri, you can't call that adorable little puppy 'Grunt!' You must choose something dignified, a name that he can grow into."

She paused for a few moments, thinking. "What about 'Henry Bartholomew Cornelius Van Buren the Third?' You know, after our long and distinguished line of great-uncles?"

Terri blanched. "Ida, what if he runs out in traffic? He'll be pancaked before I could even get his first syllable out!" But Aunt Ida was firm. No dog in her family would be saddled with an ordinary name.

A diplomatic compromise was reached and world peace was preserved. Ida was satisfied with a birth certificate that read like a family tree, and Terri got her easy, one-syllable name. Hank!

Dr. Gary Says...

Before choosing toys, ask yourself:

- Is it safe? Choose toys that are less likely to be chewed apart or swallowed. Beware of bells, buttons, and squeakers that can come loose. Removing toys surgically is both more dangerous and more costly than choosing toys carefully.
- Will it last? At least two minutes?
- Can you clean it? Yep—you should clean dog toys occasionally to keep from spreading germs to humans or other pets. Use a 10% bleach solution and dry toys completely before returning them to the chew bin.
- Is it fun? It had better be or your pooch will opt for your $100 sneakers!

Whoa! This thing is bigger than me!

So Long, Mom!

Leaving home.

It's not like when you humans part with your young. When I said goodbye, it was for good. Your kids have a way of bouncing back toting soiled laundry, various piercings, questionable soul mates and, eventually, a brand new litter.

But no pup is destined to stay with Mom and the pups forever. Terri and Ron had visited often so they weren't strangers. They were dying to take me home after just a few days, but my owner knew better. "Not before seven weeks," he insisted.

Now I know why. It gave me time to figure out what it meant to be a dog but not so much time that we'd developed a full pecking order in the litter.

The best thing I learned from my mates was where to draw the line. If I chomped down as hard as my wolf heritage allows, I'd do some serious damage. My siblings taught me how to play without hurting anyone.

Dr. Gary Says...

Deciding when a puppy is ready to take home is a bit tricky, and it varies with the breed of dog. A dog needs to pick up social skills, such as learning how hard to bite, when to quit play-wrestling, and how to communicate. A puppy left too long in the litter may become dominant and harder to train.

When it comes to feeding:

- Resist the temptation of feeding your puppy scraps and leftovers. If you start this when he's young, you may have to cook for him the rest of his life.

- Avoid canned food. It will loosen your dog's stool and make him harder to housebreak. Since canned food is about 80% water, it also ends up costing more.
- Never feed your pooch cooked bones. He can choke on the splinters or even lacerate his stomach and bowel, leading to serious life threatening infections that could require surgery.
- Don't change food brands needlessly. If you must change his food, do it gradually over a week's time by overlapping the old food with the new until the old food is phased out.

Hank's Rules

Aka *Hank Rules*

Hank must stay outside. *Say what?*

Hank can stay in the garage on very cold nights. *No way!*

Hank is allowed in the mudroom on his bed only. *I hate this.*

Hank can come into the family room but he must sleep in the corner. *That won't fly…*

Hank may get up on the old couch when we're watching TV. *Yeah, baby!*

Hank is permitted to sleep at the end of the bed. *That's better, but…*

Hank can sleep on the bed but not under the blanket. *Wait, but…*

Hank may sleep under the blanket when he's scared of thunder. *That's more like it!*

Hank can sleep in bed as long as he doesn't cut the cheese. *Sorry about that…*

Hank must give us permission to sleep in our own bed. *I love these guys!*

Puppy Tears

Remember when you brought me home, all 12 pounds of me, and laid me in my basket? Just like your own little bumpkin—oops!—munchkin.

The first night in my new home was tough. I cried and cried, all alone in my bed. Nothing smelled right. Nothing looked familiar. Well, hardly anything. At least Terri was smart enough to buy me the same food I was used to. No problems gobbling that down.

Terri, being a bit anal, thought it would help to write down my habits so that she could get to know me better. Not a bad idea, but give me a break! Look at what she wrote my first night at home:

11:00P: Go to bed.

11:06P: Can't stand Hank's crying. Get up and cradle him until he settles down.

11:21P: Up again. Poor thing, he misses his mother.

11:38P: I miss my sleep. C'mon Hank, we're right here…

11:42P: Kick Ron out of bed to tend to Hank. Pretend to be asleep as he mutters about why we ever wanted a dog.

12:07A: Police car goes flying down the street. Siren wakes him again. Remember to withhold donations to local police force.

12:41A: Decide that maybe we can't handle a real baby. Warm up some milk for our little howler and consider doggie depressants.

1:17A: Pull vet's number from Ron's wallet. Dial the first three numbers before I reconsider.

1:32A: Neighbor's dog barks. Hank starts up too. Cover head tightly with pillow.

1:46A: Push Ron violently out of bed. Threaten divorce if he complains.

2:56A: Jam in some earplugs.

3:32A: Give up! Drag Hank's bed into our room. Utter a few choice words in a sweet tone. Say a prayer.

3:45A: Is that a dog snoring?

Do you think they'll take him back?   Where's my Mommy?

How Not to Choose a Vet

Hey... woo... This isn't the way to the park!

Most of the time, I'm one happy pooch. Get to lie around all day, soak up the sun, and check my bowl hourly to see if anything new is waiting for me.

But Terri and Ron really blew it when it came to choosing my vet. I think it started to go wrong when Terri accused Ron of not doing enough to care for me. "*I'm* the one to feed him, *I'm* the one to clean up after him, *I'm* the one to walk him..." You get the idea. She may have been PMSing, but she did have a point.

So Ron takes the easy way out and uses the the Internet. "Discount pet clinics… Apprentice vets…" I heard him murmur. Rather than asking around, he chooses the vet with the biggest ad. Uh oh.

I knew this place was trouble as soon as we walked in. Ron waited at the front desk for ten minutes before anyone greeted us. Terri wrinkled her nose at the questionable odors thinly disguised by disinfectants. I picked up on the smell of fear that preceded me in the waiting room. These were not encouraging signs.

But what really turned me off was my exam. Not that I'm crazy about doctors with their rubber gloves and needles, but this guy was way too eager to get started. Something about him brought a growl right up from my bowels. Even Ron winced.

It got better after we found Dr. Gentlefingers. She actually liked dogs, rather than seeing them as another challenge. She took time to get to know me, gave me treats rather than pulling out the needle, first thing. Not that I ever liked going to see her, but at least she made it tolerable.

In fact, I was just getting used to her when Ron and Terri started talking about me having "that surgery." An operation? But I wasn't sick. What in the world could that mean?

A Vet Should Be…

- Professional
- Friendly and respectful toward you and your pet
- Happy to answer your questions
- Willing to spend the time it takes to give you and your pooch good service
- Upfront about fees and treatments

Dr. Gary Says...

Choose a vet near your home. You'll be glad you did in the event of an emergency.

In addition to a regular vet, find a 24-hour emergency veterinary clinic or ask your veterinarian to recommend one. Post this number on your refrigerator or by your telephone and in your cell phone for quick retrieval.

Ask your neighbors and friends who they recommend and check out each one to find a match. When choosing a vet, trust your instincts and pay attention to your dog. If personalities don't click, keep shopping around.

Spay or neuter your pooch. Your dog will probably live longer, be healthier, and have fewer behavior problems. You'll also be doing your part to reduce pet overpopulation.

Puppy Paranoia

What dog? Oh... that dog!

I didn't know I was doing anything wrong.

I mean, there I was, surveying my turf, standing my ground against that Siamese cat that enjoys tormenting me from the other side of the street. I guess that's why I didn't see him coming.

The dog catcher. Slipped right up behind me and grabbed my collar before I knew what was happening. Took one look at my tags and gleefully yelled "Aha! You're not legal!" as he tried to haul me to the back of his truck.

Lucky for me, Terri and Ron came running out of the house in time. "What's going on?" yelled Ron.

The dog catcher sneered at me and pointed to my tags, hollering, "Guilty!" Terri and Ron just scratched their heads, wondering what a puppy could be guilty of other than digging up a flowerbed.

"He's not legal!" he said, fully enjoying catching us in violation of the law. Heck, I didn't even know there was a law, and neither did Terri or Ron.

So Ron put on his Henry Kissinger hat and began diplomatic relations, which meant he started begging the dog catcher to let me off. The guy remained firm. There was nary a tremble in his chiseled jaw.

And as usual, it was Terri who saved the day. She invited the guy in for coffee and a plate of her best chocolate chip cookies. The guy was like butter in her palm. Pretty soon, they knew all about where he lived and how many boys he'd added to the local football team.

Thanks Terri. You kept me out of the slammer!

Dr. Gary Says...

Attach an ID tag to your pup's collar that lists your name, address, and phone number. No matter how careful you are, there's a chance your companion may become lost.

Check with your local shelter or humane society for information about local licensing requirements, where to obtain ID tags, and where to have your dog vaccinated.

Consider having a microchip implanted under your dog's skin. There's a national registry for these chips you can call 24 hours a day. Every dog pound and humane society can scan for a chip when an animal is brought in.

Follow this simple rule: **Off property, On leash**. Even a pooch with a valid license, rabies tag, and ID tag should not be allowed to roam outside of your home or fenced yard. It's best to keep your pet under control at all times.

Tripping Down Memory Lane

Scared the pee right out of me!

Remember when I was so small you could hold me in just one hand? You were so forgiving of my little accidents... at least for the first day or so.

Then there were the days when I chewed everything in sight… and a bunch of things you didn't find until years later. The newspaper. The remote control. The leg of the antique wingback chair handed down from Grandma. Electrical cords. Oops! Trip #2 to the vet. As I recall, I wasn't so lucky when I discovered the personal items Terri had tucked in the bathroom wastebasket. Surgery #1. Ouch!

Remember that Christmas when Aunt Ida brought over a poinsettia? It looked as good to me as it did to you, but for different reasons. Trip #3 to Dr. Gentlefingers. At least you learned that poinsettias aren't toxic, but they will give me a miserable tummy ache.

And who can forget when I discovered the joy of sex? About the same time you scheduled Surgery #2, wasn't it? For a few weeks, there, I had a lot of fun trying to find out who thought I was hot. The rocking chair could have cared less. Ron nearly sent me flying across the room. Still, I was certain there was someone out there just for me, and hey, a guy has to try, doesn't he?

Why Puppies are Better than Babies

- Puppies never wear diapers.
- Puppies will not heave strained carrots at your head, ever.
- Puppies don't need car seats, strollers, electric swings, binkies, highchairs, cribs, bottles, clothing, or a college fund.
- Puppies will not kick and scream at WalMart when you refuse to buy them a Snickers bar.
- Puppies never have to be told about Santa Claus or the Tooth Fairy.
- Puppies will never do bodily harm to their siblings (although they may harbor violent thoughts about the cat).

- Puppies will not grow up and give you lip, drive a car, flunk out of college, or bring home a girlfriend who shows way too much skin.

Potty Training

In my litter, I never had to worry much about when nature called. I mean, you just go when you have to go, right? No one hassled me about it so I figured it was no problem. Mom somehow took care of things.

But it became a big problem for Terri and Ron, especially when I didn't make it to the newspapers in the kitchen. Terri growled when she had to clean up after me. Ron stalked the living room, always watching to see if I was about to lift a leg.

I was one confused puppy. Just when I'd start to tinkle, Ron would holler "Hank, no!" and haul me outside, uttering words I won't repeat. What did he expect me to do? Hold on forever? Sometimes he'd stick my nose in my favorite spots, like I knew what that meant.

Terri had better luck getting through to me. She taught me that for some strange reason, she liked it when I went on linoleum. I thought carpet felt more like the great outdoors, but then what did I know?

She'd cover the whole kitchen with newspapers and herd me there about 40 times a day. If I let out so much as a dribble, she'd act like I'd won an Oscar, giving me hugs and treats, all for a little piddle! I'll never understand what makes some humans happy.

I got pretty good at going in the kitchen. But then she changed the rules and started moving my wet newspapers outside in the yard. I can't imagine what the neighbors thought as she's carrying the tinkle-stained *Times* outdoors, but then, that was her problem.

It took me awhile, but eventually I caught on. I still don't know what the big deal is with going in the house, but it's obviously a big no-no, and hey, they buy the kibble.

You have got to be kidding!

How Many Walks?

Puppies (>10 weeks)	Five to ten walks per day
Teenagers (6-11 months)	Four to six walks per day
Adults	Three to four walks per day
Senior citizens	At least three to four walks per day (incontinent dogs will need more)

Almost made it on the paper

Dr. Gary Says...

Puppies need to go out shortly after they eat, drink water, play, chew, or sleep. If your puppy's been confined to a crate overnight, take him out first thing in the morning.

Watch for signs that your pup has to go. He'll probably sniff and circle, looking for that just right spot. Pick him up and get him outside immediately.

Use a trigger word, such as "business," "bombs away," "politician," or "potty" to give your pup some idea of what you want him to do.

Stay outdoors with your puppy until he eliminates. This could take a while. If you can't wait for your puppy to go, put him into his dog crate and try taking him outside again every 15 or 30 minutes until he goes.

As soon as your puppy goes in the right place—on newspapers or in the backyard—immediately give him lots of praise and a treat so he'll know you're pleased with his behavior. Delayed praise is not effective, so witnessing him going in the right spot is important.

Most puppies prefer certain areas or surfaces to eliminate on, such as rugs or carpeting. Keep your puppy away from risky places whenever possible.

If your puppy suddenly runs out of sight, he may be looking for a secret spot to eliminate, so close doors to rooms where he may choose to sneak away.

2

Surprise! A Dog Is Not a Human!

So You Think Dogs Are Like Humans?

Can you lick yours?

Terri and Ron think I'm just a furry version of them. *Not!* But just to convince them, I put together a little test.

- Do you tinkle on your neighbor's mailbox when he gets a new car you'd like to have?
- Do you get fleas?
- When you go out with friends, do you sniff their body parts?

- Can you sleep all day and get free food without picking up checks from a government agency or living with Mom?
- Are you attracted to week-old garbage, especially on hot summer days?
- Will the neighbors look the other way if you walk around the block wearing nothing but a collar?
- Do you holler at the paperboy each time he makes a delivery?
- Do you make friends by rolling over for a belly rub?
- Do you sniff butts and crotches to learn more about a new person?

How'd you score?

If you answered "No" at least six times, you're a confirmed human.

If you answered, "Yes" seven or more times, get some counseling. You may have serious species confusion issues.

Why Bother with School When I Can't Get a Job?

Good question, isn't it? I mean, I don't have to earn a living, thanks to Terri and Ron's generosity. But I've noticed they're not so generous when I scratch relentlessly at the back door or jump all over Aunt Ida.

So even though I know I was born perfect, they decided I needed some training. Somehow the "sit and glare" routine just wasn't doing it for them.

So how do you know if a higher education is in your dog's future?

I Love my pet network… Lassie hmmmmm…

Top Ten Signs Your Dog Needs Training

10. Your puppy has learned how to activate the security system when you're away.
9. You're replacing the wall-to-wall carpeting for the third time—and your dog is only four months old.
8. You whip out a supersize lint brush to clean the couch when anyone visits.
7. Your pooch has buried so many bones in your houseplants that the floor has sprouted mushrooms.
6. Your mail carrier visits wearing earmuffs.
5. When you say, "Sit!" your dog hops on the couch with his bowl of chow.
4. Your daily walks give new meaning to the term "tar heels."

3. You've trained your husband to keep the lid down but your dog has learned how to lift it.

2. The Highway Department has honored your pup for his outstanding work digging a new sewer line.

1. Your neighbors have put up a "Beware of Dog" sign—and they don't own a dog.

Dr. Gary Says...

Didn't have time to start and follow through with basic training when your pup was a wee one? There's still hope. You can hire a professional trainer to train your dog for you.

Having an older dog-trained will cost you dollars and time instead of just patience and time. Once your dog and you are trained, you can follow through consistently at home. Life is so much better.

(However, you will learn how your pooch is trained so you can follow through consistently at home.)

Next Up on Reality TV: Choosing a Dog Trainer

THE GOOD   THE BAD   THE UGLY

Ron and Terri like to watch reality TV, although they won't admit it to their friends. Were they in for a shock when they went shopping for a dog trainer!

You see, dog trainers can be an exotic lot. Most of them think like dogs. Some of them have relationships with dogs that have lasted longer than their marriages. A few of them actually want to be dogs, and begin to grow long hair and scratch a little too publicly.

So the search began. Here are just a few of their findings:

L'Academie of Canine Etiquette, featuring Madame Pomplamousse, was a distinguished institution that catered only to poodles. She, like her charges, insisted upon wearing a coiffure and attitude that shamed her species. Ron was mortified when a single sneer induced even the most confident of pups to tinkle in the corner.

Lydia's School of Loving Lessons was a little too loose. Terri found Lydia on her hands and knees pleading with a puppy that refused to sit. She watched in horror as one feisty Rottweiler took shameless advantage by snapping off her glasses and hiding them beneath an overweight sheepdog.

Moe's School for Mutts ended up being a front for a Harley-Davidson repair shop. His specialty was teaching dogs how to survive a ride in the back of a '62 pickup—a skill I could live without. Moe liked dogs just fine, but he could have used a makeover from Madame Pomplamousse.

Ron and Terri finally settled on **Carole's Canines**. What a sweet place. I even caught Carole nibbling a dog treat one evening when we were the first ones there. My kinda girl.

That first day when all those puppies bounced in, I was in dog heaven. Playmates at last! Here was a roomful of kids my own age who wanted nothing more than to roll around and wrestle. I was certain we'd found the perfect play date.

Well, not exactly. Ron kept me on a tight leash. I nearly severed my vocal cords trying to get a noseful of those other puppies. That is, until Ron pulled out his bag of treats.

Hot dogs. He knew I'd do anything for hot dogs.

So in no time, I was sitting, staying, coming, lying down, and heeling (a little). Heck, I would have learned to fly a 747 for a package of jumbo franks.

Sounds like another reality TV show to me!

Dr. Gary Says...

When training your puppy, be firm but not physical. When you get your dog to understand what you want, life becomes ever so much better.

Physical reprimands are likely to lead to a broken spirit and simple fear instead of the love your pup offers so naturally.

Consider using a Halti or Gentle Leader collar for easier, gentle control.

The Crate: Prison or Paradise?

I can still hear Terri the day Ron brought home a puppy crate. "How can we do this to Hank?" she pleaded. "He's such a good dog. He'll think we don't love him if we put him in that thing!"

Ron just shook his head. He's the one who walked in last week after I trashed the house. What can I say? I got bored, felt lonely. At least you humans can dig into some Ben & Jerry's when you're feeling blue. I don't have such options.

It all started innocently. I ran to the window to check out the UPS guy and got all tangled up in the lamp cord. It crashed into a table and I ran like hell to get away from the chaos. On my way, I somehow managed to upset three houseplants and overturn a chair. I knew I was in for it, so I found a back corner to hide in. But my anxiety got the better of me and I ended up leaving a puddle on the floor.

So Ron laid down the ultimatum: a crate it had to be.

I was skeptical at first, but when Terri started leaving treats in there, I had to check it out. I guess my canine instincts kicked in because this place began to feel like home. At last, a room of my own.

Ahh… my "crib"

There's nothing worse than when Terri invites a gaggle of friends over and they all begin chattering and giggling. Many a husband has slunk away in such situations to a basement ball game. Now I have my crate.

If I ever find myself on the losing end of a lamp cord again, know where I'll go? Straight to the crate in a heartbeat!

Dr. Gary Says…

Used properly, a crate is a safe, effective, and humane housetraining tool. It provides your puppy with a secure, protective den—and gives you peace of mind.

Use a suitably sized crate or wire-reinforced puppy gate whenever you can't safely supervise your pup.

Make the crate a friendly place by feeding your pooch there.

Avoid punishing your dog by crating him. Brief "time outs" are fine.

Don't use the crate excessively. Your dog needs your time every day for companionship, interactive play, and exercise, regardless of his age.

When your pooch is comfortable with a crate, travel becomes a simple event.

My Weakness is Hot Dogs

Oh boy, another long-awaited visit from Aunt Ida. And a sure sign that Terri will want me to behave.

I can hear it now:

"Hank, sit."

"*Sit*, Hank!"

"SIT, you good-for-nothing overgrown hairball!"

Say what? You called me a hairball? Oh no, no, no! That's cat territory. I operate on different turf. Until you can speak my language, I'm boarding up the hearing center of my small and challenged brain and leaving town.

It's not that I can't hear. You know darned well I can tell the schnauzer next door from the cantankerous terrier on the corner from a single whimper. I just don't want to sit. It's infinitely more rewarding to tangle up Aunt Ida and watch her pop a blood vessel.

C'mon, Terri, think about it. What do you do when Ron's glued to a Jets game on Sunday afternoon? Yell at him? Like that does any good. I've watched you. You bring out a chilled brew, toast up some mozzarella sticks, and dip into your bag of feminine charms.

"Oh Honey, would you watch the baby while I go shopping?" Smile, bat your eyes, and push a tray of munchies under his nose. Poor guy doesn't even know what he's agreeing to before you're out the door.

I'm a lot like Ron. Let me spell it out.

Don't: Yell at me, plead with me, yank my chain, call me a hairball, threaten to haul me to the local shelter, or leave me locked in a room with the cat.

Do: Train me with hot dogs! Especially small tasty morsels I can gulp in an instant!

Dr. Gary Says...

Teaching and communication are what it's all about, not getting even with your pooch. Trying to whip him into shape won't work, but it may make your dog resent you.

Before you label your dog as hopelessly stubborn, figure out what's wrong. Are you sure your dog knows what he's supposed to do?

Discipline your pup while he's misbehaving, not after. That way, he'll understand just what he's doing wrong.

Use your dog's name positively. Never say, "Bad dog, Hank!" but rather, "Ataway, Hank!" Your tone of voice means more to a dog than the words you choose.

Remember that timing is everything. It's all too easy to reinforce your pup's misbehavior by giving him lots of attention at the wrong time. If your pooch gets you to respond when he jumps up on you, he's more likely to do it again and again.

In addition:

Don't get mad! Take a few minutes to cool off rather than adding the stress of your temper to the situation. Keep your voice calm and authoritative rather than harsh.

Enforce your commands gently. Telling your dog to sit three times teaches him that you're a pushover. Try giving a command once, show your pup what you want him to do, and then praise, reward, and pet. Teach your dog how to behave at home. He'll be more likely to behave well when he's around distractions, like other dogs and people.

Remember that rewards can be praise, petting, a toy or game, or food. Food works very well, especially small irresistible bits that he can gulp down fast.

When you begin training, give treats routinely when your dog responds correctly. If your dog just doesn't get it, walk away and ignore him.

Once your dog figures out what you want him to do (or not do), give him treats every so often, and occasionally, give him a jackpot of treats. If he doesn't know when that jackpot is coming, he'll keep trying to please you in hopes of getting lucky.

Taking You for a Walk

You say walk, I say run!

There's only one thing I love more than taking a walk: hot dogs. I may not be able to convince you to give me hot dogs every day, but I bet I can weasel a walk or two out of you.

Remember that cold, frosty morning when that rabbit popped out from behind the hedge? Kinda forgot that I was tethered to you. Sorry about those ice splinters in your chin. I just couldn't help myself.

And you can't expect me to remain calm and collected when a squirrel goes prancing up a tree, can you? I've never come close to catching one of those rats-in-disguise, but I'd give my eyeteeth to have a go at one.

The truth is, I think Ron and Terri could stand a bit of exercise. Terri's penchant for afternoon chocolate is giving her a little extra squeeze around the middle. And Ron's addiction to the riding lawn mower hasn't exactly given him buns of steel.

You see, running comes naturally to me. You folks would rather stroll and check out the neighbor's landscaping. Nothing is more frustrating than when you meet a friend and then spend ten minutes hanging around while I'm dying to find out who's preceded me on the next mailbox.

I keep forgetting that you poor human souls have only two legs and a sense of smell so miserable that you couldn't pick out your mate on a crowded bus. No wonder they assign Social Security numbers to tell you apart.

Dr. Gary Says...

Teaching Your Puppy to Walk Cooperatively

While your puppy is still in the play stage, put on his leash and let him drag it around for a few minutes each day.

When your puppy realizes that a leash doesn't hurt, start carrying the leash and moving in the direction he wants to go.

Say "Come" as he walks to help him understand that a walk is about both of you moving in the same direction.

If you want him to heel, make sure he is always on the same side of you.

As your dog gets older, your lessons can become more structured, longer, and filled with treats as long as he pays attention.

Training Older Dogs

If you begin training your dog when he is four months or older, you'll need to be firm but not physical.

Patiently guiding your dog's natural behavior works better than forcing your will upon him. Just give him a chance to figure out what you want so he can please you.

3

Canine
Challenges

Just Because It's Green Doesn't Mean It's Good For You

That wasn't Gatorade on the garage floor, was it?

Ron and Terri were clueless about why I was acting like I'd been sipping their schnapps until worse things started to happen. But when the backyard began to look like an intestinal experiment gone wrong, they put in a call to Dr. Gentlefingers.

Good thing they didn't wait until I'd sobered up. If they had, it might have been curtains for me.

The culprit: antifreeze. Who would have guessed something that tasted so sweet could be so deadly? I ended up on an IV for two days. It was either that or dialysis. The doc said if they had waited a few more hours, even dialysis might not have saved me.

It wasn't the first time I ate something toxic. With a confirmed chocoholic in the house, Terri was bound to leave out half a Snickers bar one night. I paid for that indulgence big time—begging to go out every ten minutes for the next two days. Luckily, I didn't eat enough to cause seizures.

And let's not forget the munchkin. He's only too eager to offer me a bite of whatever sticky gooey thing he's eating. Then he howls like a banshee when I take the whole thing. I wonder sometimes if his elevator is getting to the top floor.

Terri and Ron eventually caught on, though I was beginning to think they weren't the sharpest points in the toothpick box either. Ron made sure he didn't leave his smelly cigar butts lying around after his buddies came over for cards. Plus they made sure the baby started eating at the table more often.

From then on, Terri watched me like a hawk as she unpeeled her Milky Ways. She knows a threat to her chocolate stash when she sees one.

Dr. Gary Says...

I have surgically removed all kinds of items from dogs, including panty hose, brown-and-serve bags, a bra, towels, socks, and corncobs.

If you think, your pooch has eaten something dangerous, contact your vet or emergency veterinary service immediately.

Signs of poisoning include:

- Listlessness Abdominal pain
- Vomiting

- Diarrhea
- Muscle tremors
- Lack of coordination
- Excess salivation
- Seizures
- Fever

Be prepared to tell the vet everything you know:

- The name of the poison or item ingested
- When it was ingested
- The amount ingested
- The breed, age, sex, and weight of your pooch
- Your dog's symptoms

Pooch Poisons

- Antifreeze: Most antifreeze solutions contain ethylene glycol, which is highly toxic to dogs. Buy antifreeze that contains propylene glycol, which is safe for animals if ingested in small amounts.
- Xylitol - a sweetening agent is highly toxic to dogs. Even one stick of gum sweetened with that can kill.
- Lawn chemicals including insecticides, plant food, and fertilizer
- Rodent poisons
- Chocolate
- De-icing salt - Paw irritant; can be poisonous if licked off
- Insecticides in many over-the-counter flea and tick remedies - Choose prescription flea and tick control products, which are safer and more effective.

- Human medications such as aspirin, acetaminophen, and ibuprofen, cold medicines, anti-cancer drugs, anti-depressants, vitamins, and diet pills.

Other Things to Avoid

Human Foods: Cooked bones, onions and onion powder, alcoholic beverages, yeast dough, coffee beans and grounds, salt, macadamia nuts, tomatoes, potatoes, rhubarb leaves and stems. Chicken bones shatter easily and can choke a dog. Don't feed your dog anything moldy.

Household plants: Azalea, geraniums, dieffenbachia (dumb cane), mistletoe, philodendron, and poinsettia.

Rawhide doggie chews. These chews may be contaminated with salmonella. Offer chews only when supervising your dog, as they can pose a choking hazard as well.

String, yarn, rubber bands, dental floss. These items are easy to swallow and can cause intestinal blockages or strangulation.

Avoid toys with removable parts such as squeaky toys or stuffed animals with plastic eyes. Take the same precautions with your dog as you would with a small child.

Battle of the Bulge

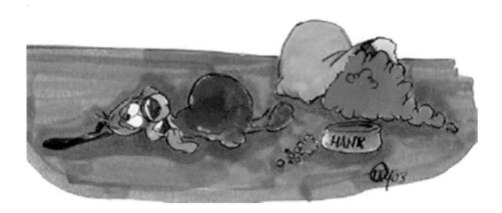

I suppose you think that fat dogs are just undisciplined beasts with no standards. Far from the truth! I live very consistently by four simple rules:

1. If it looks good, I'll eat it.
2. If it smells good, I'll eat it.
3. If it tastes good, I'll eat it.
4. If it's none of the above, I'll still give it a try.

But even with my sensible approach to food, I have developed a little extra around the middle. It first became obvious when that incredibly cute Pekinese stopped winking whenever I'd walk by. Now her head bounces like a bobble head as she watches my hind end sashay from side to side!

I'm not like you. You can just turn on the TV and see specialists practically begging you to lose weight:

"10 pounds in 10 days with the grapefruit and banana seed diet!"

"30 days to fabulous abs—just staple your stomach!"

"Eat all the pork rinds you want and still drop 20 pounds by Christmas!"

"Low-fat desserts for slimmer summer thighs!"

All that shouting about weight loss is enough to drive you to the leftover pizza, isn't it?

You no doubt carried the illusion from your childhood that an unclean plate meant starving children in Africa. So rather, than toss your leftovers, you gave them to me. Now we're both living with the result—a dog that looks like he has ingested a starving child in Africa.

Something had to change. So just like you, I went on a diet.

No more bacon slices on Sunday mornings. Banish the cheese-drenched veggies that had waited patiently in the frig for two days. All those doggie treats—gone. Even Aunt Ida wasn't allowed to sneak me the remains of her last tea cookie.

I began the slow and painful process of starvation. Is it any coincidence that "diet" without the T spells die? No amount of tail wagging, dish juggling, or brown-eyed begging would budge Terri. Instead of filling my bowl, she'd grab the leash and try to distract me with a brisk walk.

But after a few weeks, I noticed that adorable Pekinese had steadied her wobbly head as I pranced by. I think she even raised an eyebrow at me.

Maybe if I get skinny enough to wiggle out of this collar, I could take her for a vigorous fat-burning romp of the neighborhood!

Dr. Gary Says…

Provide a nutritionally balanced diet for your dog. Ask your veterinarian for advice about feeding your pup. Consider feeding food made by a company that has done extensive research.

Make sure your dog always has plenty of fresh water.

Give your pooch enough exercise to keep him physically fit (but not exhausted). Playing with your dog and walking him, twice a day is usually sufficient—and you may trim some pounds as well!

Have a high-speed breed? You'll have to get creative to get make sure your pooch gets the activity he needs. (I've seen deep paths worn along fences by some of the non-stop pups.)

Oops! Not Again, Hank!

I tried to hold it. Believe me, I really tried. But it got to the point where the only thing to do was find a remote corner, surrender to nature's call, and say a prayer that no one would notice.

Fat chance! Terri's sense of smell is fairly respectable for a human. The minute she came home, I got a look that withered my very soul—and a few choice words that I know she doesn't want the munchkin to learn.

Someone should have told Terri that having a dog means occasional cleanups. She puts up with a decorative layer of my hair everywhere, my less than gracious eating habits, and regular gaseous emissions, but she blows her top when I do it in the house. For all her worries about potty training the munchkin without doing psychological harm, you think she'd be a little more forgiving when a poor beast like me has an accident.

Guilty as charged…

Terri decided to spray the spot with a little ammonia. I figured this was the human version of marking behavior: she was covering up my scent with a whopping powerful one of her own. Doesn't that mean I'm supposed to go there?

Wow, did I catch it that time! She booted me outside for an entire afternoon and got on the phone with the vet.

That's when she hit upon an enzyme product that magically sucked up all smell. At first, I thought my sniffer was snuffed. To my dismay, my deepest inhale yielded not even the slightest trace of anything interesting. To Terri's delight, no more cleanups… at least not for a while.

Dr. Gary Says...

For wet stains on carpet: Soak up urine with a thick layer of paper towels and a thick layer of newspaper. The more you can soak up, the better.

If possible, place newspaper under the area and stand on it for a minute to soak up more. Repeat with new padding until the area is barely damp.

Rinse area with cool water and blot thoroughly or use a wet-vac.

Use a pet odor neutralizer on the spot. Test it first to make sure it doesn't create another stain.

If you don't have neutralizer, use club soda and follow the above absorption techniques.

Non-bleach bleach – Na-percarbonate releases H2O2, which will neutralize urine and fecal odors. Test before using on carpet for possible staining.

For older stains on carpet:

Rent an extractor or wet-vac to force clean water through the carpet. Don't use chemicals with these machines; they work better with water.

Try a high-quality carpet stain remover.

Avoid steam cleaners. They can permanently bond the stain and odor to carpet fibers.

Don't use chemicals with strong odors like ammonia or vinegar. Your dog may be encouraged to go there again.

Use a pet odor neutralizer on the spot. Again, test it first to make sure it doesn't create another stain.

For furniture, walls, or hardwood floors: Try enzymatic cleaners on some washable enamel paints and wallpapers.

If wood has discolored, you may need to replace a layer of varnish or paint.

Make sure any product you use is safe for pets. Test all products in an invisible area before using.

For clothing and bedding: Wash all fabric, adding about one pound of baking soda to your usual detergent.

Dry fabrics outside.

Wash with a pet odor neutralizer.

If your pet goes on the bed, cover it with a vinyl tablecloth (dogs don't like the way it crinkles).

Any of these enzyme-based products will help neutralize pet odors: Nature's Miracle®, Nilodor®, Fresh 'n Clean™, Outright® Pet Odor Eliminator.

Some stains you can smell but not see. Use a black light in a dark room and then circle the soiled areas in chalk. Black lights are commonly available at home supply stores.

The Canine Rap

When I go out, I just have to see
If another dog has been at my tree
I sniff it up and I sniff it down
Gotta get a read on the dogs around.

It's the canine rap, it's the way I tell
Who lives in the 'hood, by the way they smell
Leave my calling card, it's the way I say
I been out to walk and I passed this way.

Just a tinkle here and a tinkle there
Can't ya' tell my scent is beyond compare?

If you come around with the urge to go
I'll be back again, leave a little mo'

It's the canine rap, it's the way I tell
Who lives in the 'hood, by the way they smell
Leave my calling card, it's the way I say
I been out to walk and I passed this way.

Dr. Gary Says...

Dogs are territorial animals. They stake a claim to a particular space, area, or object. To let other people and animals know about their claim, they mark it using a variety of methods at different levels of intensity. For example, a dog may bark to drive away what he perceives to be intruders in his territory.

Some dogs may go to the extreme of urinating or defecating indoors to mark a particular area as their own. Urine marking usually is not a house-soiling problem—it's a sign of territorial behavior. To resolve the problem, you must understand why your pooch needs to mark his territory in this way. But first, take your dog to the vet to rule out any medical causes for his behavior.

If you have not spayed or neutered your pup, do so as soon as possible. Sterilizing your pooch may stop urine marking altogether. However, if he has been urine marking for a long time, a pattern may already be established.

How to Tell Urine Marking from Urinating

A dog may be urine marking if:

- He marks frequently when you walk him.
- He urinates a small amount, particularly on vertical surfaces.
- He lifts his leg to mark.
- He goes on new objects in the environment, such as a guest's briefcase or purse.

- He marks on objects with unfamiliar smells or another animal's scent.
- He has conflicts with other animals in your home.
- He has contact with animals outside your home.
- He's reacting to a new resident in your home, such as a roommate, spouse, or baby.

What To Do

Keep objects likely to cause marking out of reach. Place items such as guests' belongings and new purchases in a closet or cabinet.

Resolve conflicts between animals in your home.

Begin by cleaning soiled areas thoroughly, but don't use strong-smelling cleaners that may cause your pooch to over-mark the spot.

Restrict your dog's access to doors and windows through which he can observe animals outside. If this isn't possible, discourage the presence of other animals near your house.

Have new members of your home make friends with your pooch by feeding, grooming, and playing with him.

If you have a new baby, make sure good things happen to your pooch when the baby is around.

When Munchkin Came Along

L ife was just fine with the two of you and of course, ME. I don't know why you decided to mess it up by having Twinkle Toes.

I don't mean to offend, but this baby of yours seems pretty tedious. He sleeps all day, eats every half-hour, fills mountains of diapers, and can barely hold up his own head. I wonder if he'll ever learn to play with me or if he'll always be this helpless, hairless mammal who can't even sit up.

I'm patient by nature, but this kid has a lot to learn, like:

The proper way to greet a friendly face is not to bang it on the head with a spoon.

If he dumps his Cheerios® on the floor, they're mine, and I don't want to catch any grief about it.

He has no grounds for tears if he offers me his Popsicle and I lick it.

My tail is connected to my body and contains plenty of nerve endings.

Terri and Ron think I'm jealous because I piddle on the diaper bag. They consulted a library of dog books and decided that I wanted all the attention for myself. Nice try, but it misses the mark.

The only reason I whiz on that bag is to make sure that Babushkin here doesn't think he's master of my turf. It took me a long time to teach Terri and Ron who the boss was, and I'm not about to let some stork delivery mess it up.

If I had a chew toy for every kernel of knowledge I could pass along to you humans, I could stock my own pet store.

What a Baby Does...	**What a Dog Does,**
Follows dust particles above your left eyebrow for the first month, no matter how often you coo at him.	Follows you everywhere, even when you accidentally step on his toes.
Requires massive amounts of paper products and a Swiss bank account just to get the hang of potty training.	Learns to do his business in three days flat on old newspapers or outside.
Demands that someone look after him 24 hours a day.	Is willing to stay alone for a few hours at a time without self-destructing. (The house and furniture are another matter.)

What a Baby Does...	What a Dog Does,
Picks up ear infections within 100 feet of any sick child and lets you know for the next ten nights that his pain takes priority over your sleep.	Hardly ever gets sick and doesn't complain much when he does.
Rolls over after four months of enthusiastic encouragement from you.	Leaps six feet to pick a Frisbee out of the air and return it to you (sometimes).
Eventually learns to talk and ask you what a penis is in the checkout line at the grocery store.	Gee, I think he's got me there!

Dr. Gary Says...

Encourage friends with babies to visit your home to familiarize your pooch with babies. Be sure to supervise all dog and infant interactions.

Get your pup used to baby-related noises months before the baby is expected. For example, turn on the mechanical infant swing, and use the rocking chair. Make these positive experiences for your pooch by offering praise or a treat.

If the baby's room will be off-limits to your pooch, install a sturdy barrier such as a removable gate or a screen door. Because these barriers still allow your pooch to see and hear what's happening in the room, he'll feel less isolated from the family and more comfy with the new baby.

Use a baby doll to help your pooch get used to the real thing. You can even use the baby's name if you've selected one.

Sprinkle baby powder or baby oil on your skin so your dog becomes familiar with the new smells.

When Fleas Frolic on Fido

I'm so used to scratching and nibbling myself that another itch barely gets notice. But when a generation of fleas opened a hotel chain on my skin, it became torture.

Terri and Ron couldn't understand why I would suddenly burrow in and found it highly embarrassing when relatives were over. I had no way of telling them that there's a big difference between dry skin, a bit of harmless exploration, and an infestation of blood-sucking vampires that have targeted me as their next victim.

The biggest problem with fleas is their gestation period —about 30 minutes. Two fleas I can live with, but 200 are intolerable. In no time, those fleas had hosted a family reunion and the overflow began to spill over to the living room carpet.

I can still hear Terri's scream when she was doing her yoga and got nipped on the ankle. As if I hadn't been suffering such indignities for days! When she stood up and found one hopping on her sock, you'd have thought she'd discovered the Ebola virus right there in suburbia.

She spent the next 20 minutes trying the catch the little pest with her fingers, which I could have told her was next to impossible. Then she filled the house with so many toxic sprays that the Health Department could have declared our house a biohazard. Finally, she herded me and the munchkin outdoors and detonated a flea bomb the size of which nearly sent the nation into Orange Alert.

When the air cleared, we went in to check out the damage. It was a massacre. Entire families, generations, and bloodlines of fleas annihilated and scattered on the floor. Terri nearly clogged the vacuum trying to suck them all up.

That was the beginning of a new pill regimen for me. It was a heck of a lot easier than itching my skin raw. And I never want to see the horror that crossed Terri's face when she found the bugs in her house, not just on me.

Of course, I don't dare tell her about this tick that keeps hanging on under my armpit. She'd probably lose lunch over the thought of Lyme disease.

Why Fleas Thrive on Your Dog

Hair is an ideal place to sneak away and conceive baby fleas.

When baby fleas grow up, they can spread out and start their own subdivisions.

When flea relatives come to visit, they stay as long as they want.

Fleas will choose dogs and cats first, but they're not picky. No pup around? A human will do just fine.

When large teeth or paws begin to dig in nearby, fleas can flatten themselves and blow raspberries at your poor suffering pup.

Dr. Gary Says...

Remember the adage: For every flea on the dog, there are ten in the carpet and furniture. Fleas hop off your dog after a few days to find some other warm-blooded creature.

Use only flea and tick treatments recommended by your veterinarian. Some over-the-counter flea and tick products can be toxic, even when used according to instructions.

Newer flea medications are effective for 30 days. Another treatment is needed only if more fleas are around. New products are better, safer, and more effective than ever before. Some treatments will take care of fleas and ticks, plus protect against heartworm.

Kitty Catastrophe

What do you mean she's staying!?

How could you *do* this to me? Not only do you bring home a new baby, but you have the audacity to adopt a cat!

From Day One, that feline was the bane of my existence. During the few minutes she was awake each day, she'd settle her entire body over the heating vent and plot ways to torment me.

Remember the story about the gingham dog and the calico cat? Who fought and scratched and bit so hard that one night, they ate each other up? Well, it's not as far-fetched as you may think. I have only a few questions when it comes to cats:

- How come she can crawl on your lap at night?
- Why doesn't she have to learn how to go outside?
- How come you have a cat with Ron's allergies?
- Why do you woo her with every imaginable treat until you find a food she'll eat?

- Why do you lavish attention on her when she won't come when called, protect the house, or show any loyalty except at mealtime?

I can tolerate the occasional swipe at my legs. She can even take a drink from my bowl if the mood strikes her. But I can't stand the evil superiority that lurks beneath those languid eyelashes. She knows we're at war for our owner's attention, and I have to work far harder at getting it than her.

There's a lesson in all this for cat owners everywhere. I'll put it as simply as I can:

Canine = charming, comic, companion
Feline = fickle, fecal, fascist

Dr. Gary Says...

Like most animals (and people) that live in groups, dogs establish a social structure to maintain order, reduce conflict, and promote cooperation among pack members. Dogs also establish territories they may defend against intruders or rivals. Obviously, a dog's social and territorial nature affects his behavior when a new pet is introduced to the household.

When Introducing a New Pet

Choose a neutral location to introduce a new dog or cat. When the animals can tolerate one another without fear or aggressiveness and investigative greetings have tapered off, you can take them home.

Use positive reinforcement with encouraging talk, treats, and simple commands.

Don't allow the animals to investigate and sniff each other for too long; this may escalate to an aggressive response.

Be aware of body postures:

A dog crouching with his front legs on the ground and his hind end in the air is an invitation to play.

Signs of aggressiveness include deep growls, hair standing up on a dog's back, teeth-baring, a stiff-legged gait, and prolonged stares.

If you see unfriendly body postures, interrupt the interaction immediately by calmly getting each pet interested in something else. Try letting the animals interact again later, but this time for a shorter time period or at a greater distance from each other.

If you have more than one pooch in your household, consider introducing the resident dogs to a new pet one at a time. Two or more resident dogs sometimes gang up on a newcomer.

Support the dominant dog in your household even if he's the newcomer. This may mean, for example, allowing the dominant pooch to claim a favored sleeping spot or have access to a desirable toy.

Don't try to impose your preference for which animal should be dominant. This can confuse your pets and create further problems.

A Word about Puppies

Puppies can pester adult dogs mercilessly. Before the age of four months, puppies may not recognize subtle body postures from adult dogs signaling that they've had enough.

Well-socialized and good-natured adult dogs may set limits with puppies with a warning growl or snarl. These behaviors are normal and should be allowed.

Adult dogs that aren't well socialized or have a history of fighting with other dogs may try to set limits with more aggressive behaviors such as biting. For this reason, don't leave a puppy alone with an adult dog until you're certain the puppy isn't in danger.

Be sure to give the adult dog individual attention and some quiet time away from the puppy.

Foot Fetish

I just love ladies' shoes, don't you? Give me a brand new pair of high-rise sandals and I'll chew my way to puppy heaven. I can floss my eyeteeth with those spaghetti straps—a far cry from those pigs' ears Terri tries to push on me.

But Terri has different ideas when it comes to her shoes. She's always yanking them back, screaming, "Don't you know these cost $110 a pop!" All I know is that her shoes are nice and supple after I grind them down for a few hours.

This isn't the first time Terri and I have been at odds over her shoes. She booted me out back for the entire afternoon after I added a peekaboo hole to the toe box of her running shoes. After an hour of angry tears, an ice cream bar, and a call to her mother, Ron still got an earful when he got home.

"Look what that good-for-nothing mutt of yours did to my shoes! We give him a carload of toys and he picks the one item that costs me three days of work! Why can't he chew on all those rawhide bones we give him?"

So that's when Terri's training began. I finally got across that anything on the floor is my turf. And after a few miserable days without those red-hot high heel boots, she learned how to pick up after herself.

Crisis resolved, peace restored. The floor wasn't littered with Terri's stuff. Ron heard fewer complaints.

I wasn't tempted by the softest calf leather this side of Los Angeles. And suddenly, those pigs' ears didn't look so bad.

Are you kidding? Trade this great leather shoe for a rubber toy?!

Dr. Gary Says...

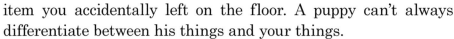

Rather than trying to stifle your puppy's chewing tendencies, direct him toward chew toys.

If you give your puppy old socks, shoes, sneakers, or articles of clothing to play with, don't be surprised when he picks a favorite item you accidentally left on the floor. A puppy can't always differentiate between his things and your things.

Teach your pup to retrieve a ball, toy, or Frisbee as a way of curbing his chewing instincts. Make training fun and filled with treats to speed the process and make it enjoyable for both of you.

Achoo!

Signs that spring is here:

- Flowers bloom.
- Grass grows.
- Ron spends two hours trying to start his riding lawn mower.
- Ron consults with his buddy John over three beers about that starter problem.
- John starts the lawn mower in five minutes flat.
- Ron mows the lawn with no shirt.
- The neighbors hurry indoors to avoid the view.
- Ron staggers into the house sneezing and wheezing for the next two days.

After popping all sorts of pills that made him dry but dopey, Terri insists he see a doctor. It turns out that Ron has allergies, not only to mold and grass and perfume, but to me!

I got scared there for a while. Ron found out that dogs that shed—like me—tickle the sinuses more than other breeds. I thought Terri and Ron were going to trade me in for a cleaner model, like a schnauzer or a poodle. How could they even think of swapping such a fine specimen of canine breeding for a wimp dog that wears bows?

Luckily, the solution was easier than that. Terri began brushing me before I came inside to get the pollen out of my coat. Ron started getting shots. He even visited an acupuncturist and was surprised how much it helped. And spring eventually found its way into summer. Before long, Ron was almost back to normal.

I still can't figure out why humans can be allergic to hair. I mean, from my vantage point, they leave it all over the house—the shower drain, wastebaskets, brushes—even on each other.

I wonder, somehow, if the cat isn't behind all this…

Dr. Gary Says...

Don't automatically assume you're allergic to your dog. Ask your allergist to specifically test for allergies to dog dander. Many people are much more sensitive to cat dander.

If you do have allergies:

- Create an allergy-free zone in your home, preferably in the bedroom, and strictly prohibit your pet's access to it.
- Use a high-efficiency HEPA air cleaner in the allergy-free zone or the entire house if you can.
- Use a micro filter bag in the vacuum cleaner to effectively catch all allergens.
- Bathe your pooch weekly to reduce the level of allergens on fur.
- Try immunotherapy (allergy shots) to improve your symptoms. Shots tend to be around 80% successful with allergies to animals, so you'll want to discuss these odds in your case.
- Truthfully, you may not be able to eliminate your allergies entirely. Consider using steroidal and antihistamine nose sprays and antihistamine pills when symptoms occur.
- Try consulting an acupuncturist who has had success relieving allergies.
- Experiment with natural products such as juice from mangosteen, which can be helpful in reducing cat allergies.

Where the Nose Goes

Who me scared?

This is a recipe for trouble, especially if I sneak beyond the yard.

When I'm loose, it's as if there's an invisible string tugging me from one scent to the next. I don't look up to see where I am. I just follow the glorious world of smell from one interesting place to another. By the time I raise my head to check my bearings, I'm clueless how I got there. Following scents back home in reverse doesn't always work.

Dr. Gary Says...

The Latest in High-Tech IDs

Take the time I found a loose board in the back gate. My first thought was to find my way to that overgrown boxer that keeps dropping greetings at my tree. But I ended up in a back alley that reeked of cat heaven. Worse yet, it began to rain.

After a few hours, this guy came out a side door and spotted me crouched behind a trashcan, trying to stay dry. I was leery of him at first. With a day-old beard and a bloodstained apron, he had all the makings of the next Freddy Krueger.

But luck was with me that day. It turns out he was a butcher! He toweled me off and brought me in the backroom; even found me a nice juicy bone. Talked non-stop about this beagle he had years ago that he'd sneak into work when the boss wasn't looking.

When Terri and Ron came for me, they nearly smothered me with hugs and kisses. Who would have guessed they cared that much?

Thank you, Ron, for the fistful of new tags you attached to my collar after my run-in with the dogcatcher. I'll never again complain about sounding like a cheap wind chime!

A Home Again or Avid chip contains identifying information and is implanted under your dog's skin. All shelters and humane societies have scanners that can trace your pet's implant back to you.

Although a high-tech approach is a great failsafe, always have your current phone number attached to your dog's collar. That's the quickest way to get your buddy back.

4

Help! I Have
a Bad Dog!

What I Wish Mom Had Told Me

- Do not mess with Ron when he's on the toilet. He does not want to engage in tug-of-war with his jockeys or play catch with that soggy tennis ball you drop at his feet.
- Do not raise holy hell when the garbage collector visits. He is not stealing your stuff.
- Do not roll your toys behind the fridge.
- Do not shake the rainwater out of your fur after entering the house—especially during Ron's nap time.
- Do not eat the cat food (before or after the cat eats it).
- Do not look for the last bit of clean carpet when you're about to throw up. And never throw up in the car.

- Do not roll on dead seagulls, woodchucks, fish, or anything else that reeks.
- Do not assume that the litter box is your cookie jar. Ditto for the diaper pail and whatever unmentionables you may find in the bathroom trash.
- Do not eat socks and then redeposit them in the backyard after processing.
- Do not wake up Terri or Ron by sticking your cold, wet nose on bare flesh.
- Do not chew anyone's toothbrush, ever!
- Do not use the sofa as your face towel. Ditto for Terri and Ron's laps.
- Do not chew crayons or pens, especially the red ones. Terri will think you're bleeding.
- Do not clamor to have the car window rolled down when it's raining. And don't bite the officer's hand when he reaches in for Ron's driver's license and registration.
- Do not bark each time you hear a doorbell on TV.
- Do not steal Terri's underwear and play hacky sack in the back yard with it.

An Avalanche of Words

What I would do to comprehend your strange and quirky language! Not that it would bring peace to the Middle East, but at least it would foster a bit of familial harmony.

Of course, I'm a highly intelligent creature. I can be trained to detect bombs, keep the blind safe crossing the street, and hang onto the arm of a suspect during an arrest. What doesn't come naturally is decoding the overwhelming array of sounds you can emit from your vocal cords.

Terri jabbers at me like I know what she's saying. Sure, I get a few words like "out" and "no," but beyond that, she could be rattling off algebraic equations for all I know.

"Wanna go for a ride, Hank?" she'll say, jangling her keys. What do I understand? Keys + door = car. I wag my tail and get excited because it puts a smile on her face, and I love to please her.

What she doesn't get is that I can't understand lengthy explanations, especially for anything that occurred more than five minutes ago. If I wrestle with a houseplant while she's at work, she'll start hollering at me hours after the fact using a cascade of words that means nothing. I'll know she's unhappy from her gestures and tone, but I won't know why.

The problem is not just too many words. It's when you choose to throw all those sounds in my direction. I live by *carpe diem*—seize the moment. I don't understand if you're upset about something I did hours ago. Catch me in the act and I get it. Otherwise, I'm hopelessly lost.

Just look at how we canines differ from you:

Dr. Gary Says...

Dogs understand whistles, voice patterns, intonations, and body language much better than specific words. If you want to train your dog to respond reliably, be consistent and firm in how you command him, and don't ever be abusive.

Call attention to bad behavior right after it occurs, not hours later. Otherwise, your pup won't know what you're trying to correct.

Quit That Barking!

I almost caused deafness, didn't I? Consider it training for when the munchkin turns 15 and starts playing Nirvana at 180 decibels.

But you know how it is. You can't tell how loud you sound. Ever listen to Aunt Ida when she whips out the cell phone to call her daughter? It doesn't matter if she's discussing Uncle Harold's neck size or how to prevent a bladder infection. Cell phones bring on a broadcast voice.

Part of the problem is my superb hearing. On good days, I've been known to distinguish a red squirrel from a gray one as they clatter up the tree. I can tell the howl of a husky from the whimper of a whippet.

Another part of the problem is the visitors. Half the reason Ron wanted me was so that no one could come in without my permission. So what am I supposed to do with this parade of strangers?

The UPS guy marches right up to the front door, leaves off packages, and scurries back to the truck. For all I know, he's a Unabomber wannabe.

Two garbage men drop by every week to haul away all that precious garbage long before my olfactory nerve is through analyzing it. If that's not burglary, I don't know what is.

So Ron decides it's time for the crate. Terri looks on nervously, certain that such cruel treatment will send me to a doggie therapist for the rest of my adult life.

If I could find some well-groomed Lhasa Apso to act as Freud, a crate would be just what she'd order. No more trying to figure out friends from enemies. I'd just lie back, order up another piña colada, and ignore that troublesome doorbell.

Yuk, Listerine! Ok, Ok! No more barking!

Dr. Gary Says...

First, try to determine why your pooch is barking.

If your dog barks because...
He's bored, lonely, or wants attention...
Try these:

- Give him more people time.
- Walk him twice a day and play with him.
- Teach him to fetch and practice a few commands daily.
- Take him to a training class.

- When you're not home, keep your pooch busy with toys that are filled with treats.
- Rotate toys to keep them interesting.

He's guarding his turf...
Try these:

- Teach your pooch the "Quiet" command (see next section).
- Have your pooch spayed or neutered to decrease territorial behavior.

He's afraid of loud noises...
Try these:

- Desensitize your dog to the sounds that bother him. (You may need professional help with this.)
- Talk to your vet about anti-anxiety medication while you work on behavior modification.

Teaching the "Quiet" command

1. When your pup begins to bark at a passerby, allow two or three barks, and then say "Quiet."
2. Immediately interrupt his barking by surprising him. You can shake a can filled with pennies or squirt water or Listerine at his mouth. This should cause him to stop barking momentarily. (You may find a pump-up squirt gun more effective to reach long distances, and Listerine seems to work the best.)
3. While he's quiet, say "Good quiet" and pop a tasty treat into his mouth.

Remember, a loud noise or squirt isn't meant to punish your pooch. It's intended to distract him into being quiet so you can reward him.

Note: If your dog is frightened by the noise or squirt bottle, find a different way to interrupt his barking, such as throwing a ball or toy near him.

What about Bark Collars?

Dr. Gary doesn't recommend electric shock bark collars because a dog may replace barking with bad behavior such as digging, escaping, or aggressiveness.

You might consider using a bark collar that gives a startling burst of citronella immediately after any bark. This will usually stop excessive barking.

Other Tips

- Keep your pooch inside when you're unable to be outside with him.
- Let your neighbors know you're working on the problem.
- If your pooch is well socialized, ask your employer if you can bring your dog to work occasionally.
- When you have to leave your dog for long periods of time, take him to a doggie day care center, hire a pet sitter or dog walker, or have a friend or neighbor walk and play with him.
- If your pup barks indoors when you're home, call him to you and have him obey a command such as "Sit" or "Down". Then reward him with praise and a treat.
- Remember to pay attention to your dog when he's being quiet so that he comes to associate such behavior with attention and praise.

Prozac for Pups

Me, afraid? Well.....

Terri likes to practice hot yoga using a tape on the TV. Gets herself into these contorted positions and then starts breathing unnaturally. The first time it happened, I was certain she was having a seizure. But after she untangled her legs, she was so relaxed she loaded me up with pup treats.

I wish I could chill out the way she does. No yoga for dogs, at least not yet.

I think I started to get uptight when the munchkin came home, and it got worse with the cat. I remember my mother as being the nervous type, always poking around to see if we were ok and pacing when it got near mealtime.

I'm unnerved by the simplest things. A car backfiring. Motorcycles. Thunder. A slammed door. All those kids at Thanksgiving. Ron flying around the corner when he realizes he's missed the first ten minutes of a game.

Since this is America, the most ambitious of you humans have hit upon dozens of remedies for nervous pups. Pet therapy. Behavior modification for owners. Puppy downers. Crates. Even luxury spas for dogs.

My favorite? The crate.

The best thing about the crate is the guilt trip it puts on Terri and Ron. They don't know that I've been stashing my well-worn puppy chews there, just waiting for a little more softening up.

Signs of a Frightened Dog

- Body postures such as a lowered head, flattened ears, or a tucked tail.
- Panting, salivating, trembling, pacing, or trying to escape.
- A huge, open-mouth smile with the cheeks drawn back as far as they will go.
- Submissive behaviors including avoiding eye contact, urinating submissively, rolling over to expose the belly, or freezing and remaining immobile.
- Barking or growling at a fearful object.
- In extreme cases, a dog may become destructive or lose control of his bladder or bowels.

Dr. Gary Says...

Most fears won't go away by themselves, and left untreated, may worsen. Some fears, when treated, will decrease in intensity or frequency but may not disappear entirely.

After you've ruled out medical causes, try to identify what triggers your pup's fear. Most fears can be treated using desensitization and counter-conditioning techniques, which require a lot of time and patience. You may need help from an animal-behavior specialist.

As a last resort, consider medication.

Jumpin' Jack Flash

The doorbell!

The one sound that will snap me out of a nap and have me on my feet in one second flat.

The glorious noise that means new scents are about to enter the room.

My siren call for a little more fun.

Aunt Ida!

Not my favorite human, but oh, how I love making her squirm when I leap at her with a big slobbery kiss!

Aunt Ida did what any self-respecting human would do. She let out a screech that wilted the houseplants. It wilted me too, and left me unable to pick up those high tones in my right ear.

So Terri started rummaging through the dog books again. Ron's contribution to the problem was to add his baritone to the melee when friends visited with an impressive, but ineffective, "Down, Hank!"

Evidently, Terri and Ida got to talking. The next time Ida came over, balancing a tray of finger sandwiches, she stomped down hard on my back toes. Yowza! Okay, I get the message! You don't have to be so rough.

Pretty soon, Terri started wooing me with those hot dogs again, getting me to sit whenever anyone came in. It worked like a charm.

Hot dogs make me forget all about the doorbell, even if our guests bring a munchkin who's easy pickings. Licking a cheek clean of leftover ice cream just doesn't compare with a fully-cooked, pop-open wiener.

Dr. Gary Says...

If your pooch will not sit on command when visitors arrive, go back to square one and train him in a quiet situation. Then gradually move his training to a more exciting arena.

If he continues to jump up during training, have your guest knee him in the chest or step on his back toes. Then have your guest turn away and ignore any more advances. This may sound harsh, but your dog will get the message in no time.

Digging and Daffodils Don't Mix

There you go again. Digging all day in your garden, setting out baby lettuce and tomatoes for an August feast. Planting a platoon of pansies that will last well into November. And ignoring me all the while.

So I did what any lonely pup would do to get your attention. I chose a central spot near the tree and turned a bit of soil of my own. I was just reaching bedrock when Ron discovered me.

Er, just trying to help you get to China…..

I was nearly traded in for another cat. Ron fretted for days about the bare patch in his otherwise perfect lawn. It set Terri to thinking, and soon Ron had another item on his "Honey Do" list: building a doghouse.

Ron spent three weekends pounding together a structure that met his architectural standards. I could have cared less about the crown molding and designer shingles, as long as it was warm, dry, and had a picture of that cute Pekingese on the wall.

By the time Ron finished, I kind of liked the spot I'd dug out under the tree, especially on those sweltering summer afternoons. I tried hammock hopping once but ended up with all four legs poking out like a trussed chicken. That cool patch of dirt was just right during those cloudless days.

We eventually reached a compromise. Ron couldn't stand that barren bit of earth messing up his landscape design, so he built a white picket fence around it and put the doghouse inside.

It was perfect. No one complained when I dug a hole under my house to cool off. Ron installed a swing door so I could check out how those green peppers were growing. And Terri mounted a sign over my abode: Hank's Haven.

Fine with me as long as I don't have to pick up the real estate taxes.

Dr. Gary Says...

Your pooch may dig to seek entertainment, attention, protection, comfort, or escape prey.

Use the same training techniques for digging as for barking.

Make unacceptable digging spots unattractive (at least temporarily). Set rocks or chicken wire in the dirt or place your dog's feces in the hole and cover it with a couple of inches of soil. Dogs don't like to dig in their own waste.

You can also try installing electric fencing a couple of inches above the ground. This method is a bit harsh but it works.

If Your Dog is a Dedicated Digger

Don't fight it! Some breeds are born diggers.

For your own peace of mind, provide an area, covered with loose soil or sand, where it's okay for your dog to dig.

If you catch your pooch digging in an unacceptable area:

- Interrupt the behavior with a loud noise and say, "No dig."
- Immediately take your pup to his designated digging area.
- When he digs in the approved spot, reward him with praise.
- Make the acceptable area attractive by burying safe items for your pooch to discover.

Booty-scooting the Carpet

You can't imagine the itch. The torment. *The sheer agony.* There's only one thing to do.

Squeegee my butt across your carpet. Sure beats toilet paper when you don't have opposable thumbs!

Actually, I don't do this to drive you nuts. I usually display such repulsive behavior to empty full anal glands, something you humans don't have (count your lucky stars). And there's no way I can take care of it without a little help… usually from your carpet.

I don't do this to gross you out, although it has proven a sure-fire way of getting unwanted visitors out of your house. I'd much rather have you smile and give me a friendly pat than scold me to stop. I just don't have your social conscience. When you get that embarrassing itch, you excuse yourself to go scratch in private. I could care less if you watch.

So what options do you have?

- Holler at me, which is absolutely useless but may make you feel better.
- Shoo me outside, if you get to me in time.
- Have the vet teach you how to take care of my problem. (Once you learn how, you'll understand why you pay good money to have it done for you.)
- Ask the vet about an operation, especially if you're dealing with this more than once a month.

Oh no . . . not another operation . . . !

Ruling the Roost

It's a dog's life.

I knight thee "Sir Pooper Scooper!"

What could be better than sleeping on the bed and eating for free in exchange for my total devotion? Ron and Terri were pushovers for a pair of "starving puppy" eyes whenever I followed them into the kitchen. Best of all, they actually encouraged me to hop on the couch and keep their feet warm on those cold winter nights.

Things would have been fine if munchkin hadn't appeared. They never complained about my getting away with murder until I left a harmless little wet spot on the baby's diaper bag... and another on the side of his crib. Oh yes, and a third dribble in his car seat. How else could I teach the newbie where he ranked in the pack?

One thing you can count on is that a dog has to know where he stands. It's not so different from humans in the vast hierarchy of any corporation, except we canines don't need MBAs to partake.

Just last spring, there was Ron looking up and down the street at all the other men sprinkling fertilizer and grass seed on their lawns. Decided he had to do it too, just to keep up. So he returns from Home Depot with two tons of lawn enhancers and spends a month making sure his lawn is as weed-free as every neighbor in the tract.

When I mark my territory, I'm doing the same thing: making it clear who's the boss. There's no way I'm going to allow a little bundle of burps to claim my turf.

Of course, it was Terri who made a fuss. "That stupid dog peed on the diaper bag! Can you believe it? What's wrong with him?!"

On the advice of Dr. Gentlefingers, Terri booted me off the bed at night. My sleep was ruined! That bed became a battleground. Every time she went away, I'd get back up on the bed where I belonged.

This went on for some time until her superior cranium dreamed up a way to foil me. A tablecloth. Yup. One of those vinyl-backed jobs that crinkle when you get up on it.

It did the trick. That bed just wasn't the cozy place it used to be. Don't tell the pups down the street, please. I couldn't stick my head out the door if they knew I was defeated by a tablecloth.

Dr. Gary Says…

To keep your home safe and happy for all residents, humans should assume the highest positions in the hierarchy, particularly with dominant dogs.

This can be done early without severe physical interaction. If you're trying to re-train an older dog, you'll have to be consistent and persistent.

The Cat in the Hat Doesn't Visit Dogs

When you close the door to go out for the day, The Cat in the Hat does not ask me to play. Thing One doesn't come with a Frisbee for me, And I'm left all alone seeking some company.

I wish I had a kibble for every time I've missed you and tried to fill the long hours until you got home. My small but gifted brain can't understand overtime, debt, Happy Hour with your buddies, or getting ahead in the world.

Left to my own devices, I came up with a bunch of distractions—and learned some valuable lessons:

- A chair leg is worth a good chew, even with the splinters. But sprayed with bitter apple, it's about as attractive as earwax.
- Barking is great for increasing lung capacity, but Ron's friends stopped inviting him over for a pre-dinner brew. He ended up at home glaring at the TV and me.
- There's one guaranteed way to attract human attention. Tinkle. In all the wrong places.

That did it. Ron and Terri brought me to Dr. Gentlefingers. When everything checked out normal, she started asking questions. It had never occurred to them that I was lonely.

Ron started whining about his job and the huge mortgage Terri made them get. Terri complained it was about time Ron got that promotion he'd been promised. The two of them hissed and gathered steam until Dr. Gentlefingers quietly came up with the perfect solution.

The radio. Now they leave it on all day so it feels like someone is talking to me.

I've become a talk-show addict. NPR Morning Edition and Fresh Air in the afternoons. The only time I howl is during the Star-Spangled Banner during games—and the neighbors are used to it.

Dr. Gary Says...

Signs of loneliness are destructive behavior when you're not home, excessive barking, urine marking, or chewing.

Learning to Play with the Dentally Challenged

You wouldn't know it to look at me now, but I was once a 98-pound weakling. In dog terms, that's a ten-pound wimp.

How I envied one of my brothers. Nicknamed "Van Damme" from birth, he was the pick of the litter—a gregarious, chubby pup that ripened into an irrepressible bundle of muscle and play.

I learned early on that what you lack in size, you make up for in charm. Van Damme took a liking to me and let me nose in for more time at Mom's round-the-clock dairy, which helped to pack on the flesh.

It turns out he was fattening me for the kill. On the day I could finally hold my own, he began teaching me all the dastardly wrestling techniques he was famous for.

Van Damme was a good pup, but he didn't know when to stop. Only a nip on the neck from Mom could get his attention, even if I'd been whimpering forever for a break in the action.

So I never learned for myself when enough is enough —that is, until it became a problem for Ron, Terri, and the seven-year-old boy next door. To make his life interesting, this kid would dart in and out of my territory, poke sticks at me, and generally get me all riled up until I'd lunge for him and get zapped.

It drove me crazy, and the crazier I got, the more he enjoyed it. He continued to force my hand until I showed him what I'd learned from Van Damme. I went flying through the invisible fence and tackled him, grabbed him by his shirt, and started rolling him around the yard.

His mother came to the rescue with a barrage of curses and a garden rake, and I took off. Terri found me huddled under an arborvitae two blocks away, shivering in fear that I'd bought myself a trip to the shelter.

A neighborhood summit was held to decide the fate of our suburban world. The boy and I stayed well clear of the fence, blaming one another for starting World War III.

At last, a resolution was passed. The kid would no longer tease me, and I would no longer stay outside for hours without supervision. Peace at last.

I only wish Van Damme could have seen me take that kid in hand. He would have been pleased to know that all his training was not in vain.

Dr. Gary Says...

When you or the kids play too rough, your pooch may nip, thinking this is part of the fun and games. If your pooch gets too rough, pull him down on the floor, say "No," and try to calm him.

Tug-of-war games train your pooch to take something and run with it. Sometimes he'll bring it back, but not always. You may reconsider engaging in such games the first time your pup takes off with your child's new baseball glove.

Training a "Jailbreak" Dog

How can you teach your dog not to run out the door as soon as you open it? Remember, dogs are like kids. If they run for it and you chase them, they'll think it's a game.

One option is to leave the door open and don't do anything. More than likely, your pooch will return on his own, wondering why you're not chasing him down the street. If that doesn't work, try this:

- Tie a 15-foot nylon line to your dog's collar.
- Securely fasten the other end to yourself or something nearby that will not give.
- Just before your pup reaches the end of the line, say "Whoa" or "Stop."
- When the line brings him to an abrupt stop, tell him to sit and praise him for being such a good dog.

5

Home and Away

Road Trip

Shotgun!

Remember that cross-state trip we took when the munchkin was only a year old? With him strapped in the car seat, out of reach of my ears and tail, I was free to roam about the extra seat in the back.

It went pretty well until we hit Maryland. That's when I started feeling a bit queasy. How can I tell you humans that? I kept hoping it would go away, but before I knew it, there was breakfast—and lunch—all over the back of poor munchkin's head.

Inside I was laughing up a storm and feeling less nauseated too. The baby was howling and Terri started hollering at Ron to pull over. A few swerves on the interstate and we were at the nearest rest stop for cleanup.

That was the last time I rode without my beloved crate.

Still, all that motion got to me. I tried focusing on the horizon but there was too much else to check out. Even a ten-mile trip had me upchucking. Dr. Gentlefingers, as usual, came up with a solution: doggie meds. Calmed me enough so I could practically sleep through.

Ron and Terri were smart enough not to leave me in the car on a hot day. But I'll never forget the time they thought I'd enjoy a trip to the local carnival. No rides for dogs, dribbled ice cream covered with ants, and fireworks at the end of it all. Yeah, right—just the things I like to do.

The one thing they forgot about was the pavement. Darn near singed the pads right off my feet! They kept thinking all that dancing was from the excitement. Wrong! I was just trying to get off the asphalt.

This year, Ron and Terri left me home for the day with a new treat and *The Prairie Home Companion* on the radio. When they got home, my toy was broken in and I knew more than I needed to know about making pickles.

Dr. Gary Says...

When traveling, take along your pup's medical records and a health certificate from your vet, indicating that your dog is in good health. If you're traveling across state lines, bring proof of a recent rabies vaccination as well.

Dogs may travel freely throughout the United States as long as they have proper documentation. Hawaii requires a 30- or 120-day quarantine for all dogs and cats, but regulations vary by species, so check prior to travel.

If you're traveling to Canada, you must carry a certificate issued by a vet that clearly identifies the animal and certifies that the dog has been vaccinated against rabies in the last three years. Different Canadian provinces may have additional requirements. Be sure to contact the government of the province you plan to visit.

If you're traveling to Mexico, you must carry a health certificate prepared by your vet within two weeks of the day you cross the border. The certificate must include a description of your pooch, the lot number of the rabies vaccine used, proof of distemper vaccination, and a vet's statement that the animal is free from infectious or contagious disease. This certificate must be stamped by an office of the U.S. Department of Agriculture. (There is a fee for the stamp. These certificates are usually good for 30 days from their date of issue.)

Home Alone

The bad news:
You're going on vacation again… without me!

The good news: You've decided to hire a pet sitter rather than leave me in a kennel with a bunch of strange dogs.

The last thing I wanted was to be cooped up in some airplane cargo bin, so I'm glad you left me home. But you could have chosen a better pet sitter.

I know you wanted someone nearby and that kid from down the street seemed ideal. Far from it. Jake would come in every morning wearing his headphones, not even glancing my way as he went about filling my bowls. I'd wag and flash my best doggie-smile, and the best I ever got was "Hey, dude."

While I did my business, he'd jive to his tunes as if I wasn't even there. I can see why you humans aren't too fond of the teen years. By the way, who's Eminem and what do those words mean?

Then there was Aunt Ida. She was even worse, if that's possible. She was so worried about collecting a little dog hair on her skirt that she shooed me away, saying, "Now Hank, be a good dog." A good dog? I was starved for a little affection and she was barely civil with me.

The woman could stand to loosen up and a friendly dog kiss might be just the ticket.

Finally, Terri took control and got a bona fide pet sitter. Butch even boasted a certificate in "advanced dog surveillance," a sure sign that this guy took the job seriously.

Butch was of the philosophy that dogs need company and exercise, and he ran me like a kindly drill sergeant.

- Arrival: Ten minutes of petting, happy talk, and grooming
- Mission 1: Fill the bowls, check the house, and water the plants
- Mission 2: Four-mile jog around the neighborhood at a brisk clip
- Mission 3: Review of training commands, including the difficult-to-master "Come!"
- Departure: Five minutes of belly rubs

By the time Terri and Ron got home, Butch had me in tip-top shape.

Of course, it didn't take long before I slipped into my old habits—sleeping all day, begging for pork rinds, and waiting to hear a command three times before budging. If you think I'm tough, wait until munchkin turns 14!

Dr. Gary Says...

A good pet sitter should:

- Be happy to see your pup and greet him lovingly.
- Know how to care for your dog, including any special needs he may have.
- Give your pooch plenty of daily exercise.
- Be on the lookout for signs of illness or conditions that require medical attention.
- Know how to contact you at all times.
- Be reliable.

Finding a Pet Sitter

Get recommendations from friends, neighbors, your vet, the humane society, or a dog trainer. Google "Pet Sitting Services."

Contact the National Association of Professional Pet Sitters (800-296-PETS, www.petsitters.org) or Pet Sitters International (800-268-SITS, www.petsit.com) for recommendations. Both organizations offer pet-sitter accreditation to those who demonstrate professional experience, complete pet-care study courses, attend professional conferences, and abide by their codes of ethics.

Check Me In at the Ritz

Choosing the right kennel is hardly akin to mastering astrophysics. To make it easy for you, just compare these two lists.

Remember, you've got your vacations… don't forget about mine!

Good Kennel

A good kennel offers the latest in canine luxuries, such as:

- Kinesthetic massage therapy for sexy, supple dewclaws.
- Teeth whitening for that brilliant smile the lady dogs can't resist.
- Jacuzzi® filled with flea dip in raised bone-shaped tubs.
- Unlimited bacon on Sunday mornings.
- Heated grooming brushes to whisk away months of dandruff.
- The latest in aerobic workouts with a personal trainer named Lance.
- A sunbaked patio, complete with awnings, a digging pit, and umbrella-studded water dishes.
- Private therapy sessions to overcome obesity and fear of felines.

Bad Kennel

A bad kennel raises your suspicions right from the start:

- 80-pound bags of chow purchased at a "seconds" discount store.
- A bare concrete floor to sleep on (your prisons look better).
- No place to do some cardio.
- A little rack over the kennel drain where the staff can hose everything out right from under me.
- Kennel cough that rivals the SARS epidemic.
- Free fleas for all residents.
- Cats placed strategically close to torment me and cause my kennel mates to howl themselves hoarse.

Dr. Gary Says...

Search the Internet for "Kennels & Pet Boarding" for a list of kennels in your area. Once you have a list of names—even ones you picked up from reliable sources—it's time to do background checks.

Find out if your state requires boarding kennel inspections. If it does, make sure the kennel you're considering displays a license or certificate showing that the kennel meets mandated standards.

Ask if the prospective kennel belongs to the American Boarding Kennels Association (ABKA, 719-667-1600, www.abka. com), a trade association founded by kennel operators to promote professional standards of dog care. Besides requiring members to subscribe to a code of ethics, ABKA offers voluntary facility accreditation that indicates a facility has been inspected and meets ABKA standards of safety, professionalism, and quality of care. Check with your Better Business Bureau (www.bbbonline. org/consumer/) to see if any complaints have been lodged against a kennel you're considering.

If boarding at a veterinary hospital, ask to see the kennel area when you're checking out the facility. If the owners are unwilling to show you where the animals are being kept, be careful.

Goodbye Starter Home

I should have known something was up when Ron brought home a truckload of cardboard boxes and then another load the night after.

Hey, where does Bubba think he's going?

It didn't take long before Terri was packing up everything in sight except the baby and me.

We were having a great time playing hide-and-seek among the boxes, when suddenly, the doorbell rang.

The movers! What an interesting collection of humanity.

Consider **Frank**. Built like a whiskey barrel, smelled like a whiskey barrel, and sported some fascinating scents on his shirt I couldn't quite place. Maybe whiskey.

Then there was **Tim**, whose arms stretched nearly to his knees. He acted like the top dog, grunting out orders under a haze of cigarette smoke that even I found stifling.

Lastly, in walks **Seth**. He tried to get friendly with me way too fast and sent me into the corner pacing and growling.

My job, as set forth in the annals of human-canine history, is to protect. From my perspective, these guys were there to pack up the munchkin and carry him away in a big truck.

Once again, Terri showed her brilliance. She'd thoughtfully moved my crate to the powder room where the only thing left hanging was a thin roll of toilet paper. She gently closed the door and kept those thieves at bay.

When we finally got to the new house, it looked like the old house—boxes everywhere—but it smelled way different. I spent the next two months trying to figure out how Berber carpets smell and customizing them to meet my rigid standards.

At least one thing hadn't changed. My competition— the baby—was lying in wait for me, ready to bite my tail just as I was sorting out how tile grout smells sweeter than concrete. Yikes!

Dr. Gary Says...

Planning ahead will make your move less stressful for you and your pooch.

- Invest in a sturdy, high-quality dog carrier to keep your dog secure and help make your car trip safe.
- Have your pup spend several nights in his crate if he doesn't yet realize that this is his den. It will make him much more comfortable when he travels.
- Purchase a new ID tag for your dog as soon as you know your new address and telephone number.

- Consider having an ID chip implanted under your pup's skin.
- Never leave your pooch alone in a parked vehicle, especially in warm weather. High temperatures inside a car can injure or kill your dog in a much shorter time than most of us realize. In any season, a dog in a parked vehicle can be harmed or stolen.
- Never put your dog in the trunk of a car, the open bed of a pickup truck, or the storage area of a moving van.
- Find hotels in advance. Online listings of dog-friendly hotels will help you find overnight lodging during your move.
- If you plan to travel with your dog by air, check with your vet, the U.S. Department of Agriculture, and the airline for regulations.
- Depending on your destination, your pup may also need additional vaccinations, medications, and health certificates.
- If your pooch doesn't enjoy car rides, consult your veterinarian about behavior modification or medication that might lessen the stress of travel.

In Your New Home

- Take with you all the things your pooch will need in your new home: food, water, medications, a bed, food and water bowls, and health records.
- Have a recent photo of your dog on hand, in case he becomes lost.
- Be patient and understanding, and provide lots of affection.

When Goodbye is Forever

We've had some wonderful years, haven't we? It's been a great nostalgic trip looking back, remembering all the good times and the hours we laughed and played. I'd like it to go on forever, but in the circle of life, we all get to play our part and move on.

Chances are, I'll be the first to go. I know there will be some pain involved, and I wish there were something I could do to make it easier. One of my greatest joys while I was alive was putting a smile on your face.

I ask only one thing in return for my unconditional love and loyalty. When my time comes, try to be wise enough and strong enough to know if I'm suffering and allow me to leave this world with dignity and grace.

Make that two things. I don't want you to mourn forever. When you're up to it, get a new puppy and start all over. Nothing heals a broken heart faster than the bright eyes of a youngster inviting you to play. You gave me enough love for several lifetimes, and I was lucky to be part of your family. But I'd be very sad if you were to continue to dwell on losing me.

Well, maybe three things. When you visit my favorite places, remember me fondly. I'll be doing the same about you, wherever I may rest.

We've spent years trying to figure out one another and getting used to each other's quirks. But through it all, we've loved each other in a way that transcends our species and even the inevitability of death.

Dr. Gary Says...

When your beloved pooch dies, it's not unusual to feel overwhelmed by sadness. Your dog provides companionship, acceptance, emotional support, and unconditional love during his time with you.

Understanding the bond you have with your dog is the first step toward coping with your loss. It's okay to grieve, however long it may take. When you are ready, another animal can bring new joy—and a new personality—into your life.

Lastly, remember that no matter how hard it is to accept the loss of your companion, it's nowhere near the joy you shared throughout his life.

The Four Stages of Grief

Let yourself go through all four stages of grief, beginning with denial, particularly if you lose your pet unexpectedly.

Denial may start before the loss of an older pet and can prevent you from allowing him to pass with dignity.

Anger often follows denial. There's nothing wrong with feeling anger, but over time, it can be destructive to your well-being. Let go of this feeling as soon as you can.

Bargaining is a stage in which you ask a higher power to bring your pooch back (and make the pain go away) in exchange for outrageous promises.

Acceptance is the last stage in which you begin to move on with your life.

6

Questions,
Anyone?

This section contains answers to common questions posed to Dr. Ailes. We hope they will answer any questions you may have.

Which dog is best suited to a family?

First determine the role a dog will play in your family's daily life. What's your lifestyle like? How much time do you have to care for your pet? How large is your living environment? And what do you want from this new relationship?

Then discuss your desires with your veterinarian and several dog breeders.

What if I'm bitten by a dog?

If you're bitten or attacked by a dog, try not to panic! Immediately wash the wound thoroughly with soap and warm water. Then contact your physician for additional care and advice.

Report the bite to your local animal care and control agency. Tell the animal control officer everything you know about the dog, including his owner's name and address. If the dog is a stray, explain what he looked like, where you saw him, whether you've seen him before, and in which direction he was headed.

Dr. Gary also says to teach your children:

- To respect dogs
- To never chase or tease any dog
- To avoid dogs they don't know

What if you're attacked by a dog?

- Never scream or run.
- Remain motionless with your hands at your sides.
- Avoid eye contact with the dog, or lie down and curl up into a ball.

If a dog attacks, push your jacket, purse, bicycle, or another item between yourself and the dog. If you fall or are knocked to the ground, curl into a ball with your hands over your ears and remain motionless. Any screaming or rolling around will keep the dog interested in you.

Once the dog loses interest in you, slowly back away until he is out of sight.

What about health insurance for my dog?

Not a bad idea. In 2021, expect to spend between $1,100 and $3,200 during the first year, the ASPCA estimates. That includes the adoption fee, the cost of spaying or neutering your pet (if it wasn't already done), food, vaccinations, supplies, bedding and crates.

For more information, Google "Pet Insurance" or check out Veterinary Pet Insurance (www.petinsurance.com, 800-USA-OETS) and Premier Pet Insurance (www.ppins.com, 877-774-2273).

Why do male dogs "get friendly" with other dogs—male or female—even though they're neutered?

Dogs do this regardless of their sex to show dominance.

What if I have to find a new home for my dog?

Shelters and humane societies are the first places to try. If you have a specific breed, contact rescue or adoption organizations that find loving homes for such dogs— and sometimes care for them until a suitable place can be found.

Try contacting friends, relatives, and your vet for placement options. Always visit the home first to make sure your dog won't be passed on to a dealer for resale —and to be certain the environment meets your dog's needs.

What if I die first?

Contact friends or relatives who will care for your dog if something unexpected happens to you—and then take the time to teach them what your dog requires.

Make sure your neighbors and friends know how many dogs you have and whom to contact if they need care. Consider making formal, written agreements with caregivers that explain what will happen if you're not around to care for your pet.

We travel internationally. Do I need a passport for my pooch?

Each country has regulations for required health certificates. Check online or with the country's consulate to get the specifics.

Don't forget to pack your dog's supplies, including food, bottled water, dishes, bedding, leash, collar, and tags, grooming items, a first-aid kit, and any necessary medications.

How can I get a good photo of my dog and me?

Put a dab of honey on your cheek and let the dog know where it is—or get down on all fours yourself. Use some of your dog's favorite toys or games to get your pooch excited if that's what you want to see in the picture.

You may consider using music or people to get his attention depending on the shot you want.

Is it okay for my dog to ride in the back of a pickup?

While this may look like fun, it's extremely dangerous for both your pup and other motorists.

Consider what can happen if your truck hits a bump, you brake suddenly, or you swerve to avoid an obstacle. Your pooch can easily be thrown onto the road and into the path of other cars. Other drivers may cause an accident by swerving to avoid hitting your dog.

It's not safe for your pooch to ride in the bed of a pickup even with a restraint—and no harnesses have been proven safe for this. In fact, there have been cases where dogs restrained by leashes or harnesses have been strangled or dragged after being thrown from a truck bed.

If you must transport your pooch in a pickup truck, put him in the cab with you in a pet carrier. If you have an extended cab, have your pooch ride in the back portion of the cab where he will be away from the front windshield.

You can build a cage in the back and know your dog is in relative safety unless there is a major accident. Your pooch also can be cross-tied in the center of the pickup bed so he can't reach the sides while in his harness. It's not quite as safe but will work in a pinch.

Printed in the United States
by Baker & Taylor Publisher Services